D1526403

Lincoln's Birthday

A CROWELL HOLIDAY BOOK

Lincoln's Birthday

By Clyde Robert Bulla

Illustrations by Ernest Crichlow

THOMAS Y. CROWELL COMPANY
NEW YORK

CROWELL HOLIDAY BOOKS

EDITED BY SUSAN BARTLETT WEBER

Lincoln's
Birthday

Abraham Lincoln was the sixteenth President of the United States. February 12 is his birthday. He was born in Kentucky in 1809.

Our country was young then. Most of the people lived in the East. But many were moving toward the West. They were making roads through the forests and building homes where only Indians had lived before.

The Lincolns were farmers in the new state of Kentucky. There were four in the family—Tom and Nancy Lincoln and their children, Sarah and Abraham. They lived in a log cabin.

Tom Lincoln had never learned to read, and he could barely write his name. Nancy Lincoln had had no more education than her husband. Abraham was sent to school before he was six, but he never went for long. Terms were short in the schools nearby, and he was often kept at home to help with the farm work.

When Abraham was seven, the Lincolns moved to Indiana. They had heard that the land was better there.

Abraham and his father cut logs and built a rough kind of shed. This was the family's home while they cleared land for a field and garden. After a year they built a cabin.

The new home had only one room, with a loft above. Abraham slept in the loft, on a bed of dry leaves.

In those days the family had few comforts, and there was hard work for all. Abraham cut wood and carried water. He plowed fields and pitched hay. Sometimes he worked on a neighbor's farm for twenty-five cents a day.

After fourteen years in Indiana, the family moved farther west, to Illinois.

Abraham's mother and sister had died. His father had married again. Tom Lincoln's second wife was a widow with three children of her own. She was kind to Abraham. He never forgot her kindness.

Abraham Lincoln had grown tall and thin. Hard work had made him strong.

In Kentucky, Indiana, and Illinois there were few schools and schoolmasters. But in the short time Abraham had gone to school, he had learned to read and write. He had learned spelling and arithmetic. At night, by the fire, he read and studied, and his stepmother did what she could to help him.

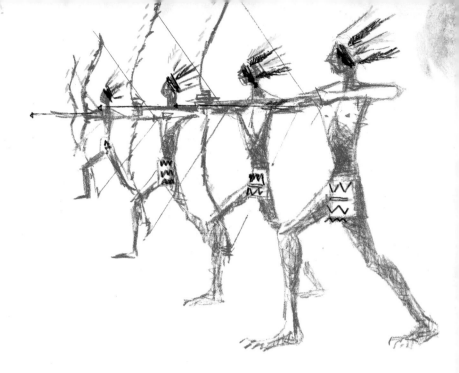

One spring he rode down the Mississippi River on a flatboat. He went as far as New Orleans. On the trip he made friends with a man who owned a store and mill in New Salem, Illinois. When Abraham came back from New Orleans, he went to work for his friend.

The next year an Indian war broke out in Illinois. White settlers were living on land claimed by an Indian tribe. Chief Black Hawk, with five hundred braves, crossed the Mississippi and tried to take the land.

The settlers raised an army of fighting men. Abraham Lincoln was among them. He was made captain of his company, and he and his men marched after the Indians. For almost three months they marched, but they never fought a battle. They were never close enough to the Indians even to see the chief and his braves.

Black Hawk was driven back, and the war ended. Lincoln went home to New Salem.

He knew everybody in the little town, and everyone knew him. People liked Abe Lincoln, and they trusted him.

He had a slow, quiet way of talking. People listened to his stories. They laughed at his jokes. Yet even when he joked, there was a sadness about him.

Some of his friends wanted him to run for public office. He ran for a place in the state legislature. He made speeches and met hundreds of people, but he did not win the election.

In the next election he ran again. This time he was elected.

For years he served in the legislature that helped govern Illinois. He became a lawyer in the town of Springfield, not far from New Salem.

He met Miss Mary Todd and married her. She had come from Kentucky to live in Springfield. She had been educated at a well-known school in the South. Her life had been far different from his.

Before they were married, and afterward, she was jealous and quick-tempered. Much of their life together was unhappy.

Four children were born to them. All were boys.

Lincoln was elected to the United States Congress. While he was in Congress, he lived in Washington. He made many friends there, and many people heard his speeches.

Then his term in Congress ended, and he went home to Springfield. He thought he would live there and be a lawyer for the rest of his life.

But he was often called away from Springfield to speak on the question of slavery. This was the great question in the country—was slavery right or wrong?

Lincoln believed it was wrong. He spoke out against it. New states were being added to the Union. He tried to keep slavery from spreading to the new states.

In 1860 it was time to elect a new President. All through the North people had begun to say that Abraham Lincoln should be the next President. All through the South they were saying that Lincoln must *not* be President.

The Southern states were slave states. Southern people wanted to keep their slaves. They wanted slavery to spread to other states, and they knew Lincoln's stand against slavery.

At first Lincoln had not wanted to run for President. He told his friends he was not fit for such a high office. But once he was in the race, he fought hard to win.

The election was held. The votes were counted. Abraham Lincoln was the winner.

ELECT

ABE

The South feared its rights would be taken away. One Southern state left the United States, and then six more. Later they were followed by four others.

Lincoln believed that no state had the right to leave the Union. The Southern states believed they *did* have the right to leave and form a separate nation.

So the North and South made ready for war —a war between the states.

Lincoln became President in March 1861. In April the Civil War began.

It was a long and terrible war. When it was over in 1865, the North had won. North and South were still one country, and the slaves had been set free.

Lincoln was still President. In 1864 he had been elected to serve another four years. More than any other man, he had held the country together. Because of him, the slaves were free.

But the war years had been almost too heavy a load for the President to bear. Thousands of his countrymen had been killed on the battlefields. Many more had been wounded. In the second year of the war, his young son Willie had died.

Now he tried to look ahead to better times.

Five days after the end of the war, he and his wife went out with friends. They went to a play in Ford's Theater in Washington.

While they watched the play, a young actor came into the theater. He was John Wilkes Booth, an enemy of the President. He believed Lincoln was a tyrant who deserved to die.

The President and Mrs. Lincoln and their friends were sitting in a theater box. Booth came up behind them. He pointed a pistol and shot the President.

He ran from the theater, but he did not escape for long. A few days later he was tracked down and killed.

The wounded President was taken to a house across the street from the theater. There, the next morning, he died.

Abraham Lincoln was gone. But his work was left.

His words were left, too, for all to read. There were his speeches on the question of slavery. There were the letters he wrote. There was his address given at Gettysburg, Pennsylvania, at the graves of men who had died in battle.

In 1866, the year after Lincoln's death, his birthday was celebrated in Washington. The celebration was held in the Capitol. The new President, Andrew Johnson, was there, with other men high in the government. There was solemn music, and there was a prayer. Then the people who had gathered listened to a speech about the life of Lincoln.

On the same day, a group of people called the Lincoln Association met in Jersey City, New Jersey. They made plans to meet each year to celebrate the birthday of Lincoln.

Twenty-two years after Lincoln's death, there was a public celebration of his birthday—a dinner given by the Republican Club in New York City. From that time on, many other public celebrations were held in honor of Lincoln's birthday. Sometimes there were dinners; sometimes there were parades; and always flags were flown.

In 1891 a dinner was given by the Lincoln Club in New York City. Hannibal Hamlin went from his home in Maine to speak at the dinner. He had been Vice President when Lincoln was President. In his speech he asked that Lincoln's birthday be made a national holiday.

The next year February 12 was made a legal holiday in Illinois. Schools and businesses were closed on this day.

In 1896 February 12 was made a legal holiday in four more states—Washington, New Jersey,

New York, and Minnesota. Today Lincoln's Birthday is a legal holiday in most of our states.

Each year the United States Congress observes the day by reading from Lincoln's writings.

On February 12 many visitors stop at the place where Lincoln was born. The little log cabin stands near Hodgenville, Kentucky.

Others celebrate by visiting New Salem, Illinois, where Lincoln lived when he was a young man. The village had been founded in 1829. For a few years it was a busy place. Then another town grew up close by and the people began to move there. Soon no one was left in New Salem.

Seventy-five years passed before a group of people in Illinois decided to build another New Salem as a memorial to Lincoln. The state government voted money to help with the work. Today New Salem stands in its old place. The village, with its tavern and stores and log cabins, looks very much as it must have looked when Lincoln lived there.

Many statues have been made of Lincoln. One of the finest is in the Lincoln Memorial in the city of Washington. It was done by the American sculptor, Daniel Chester French. Many people celebrate Lincoln's Birthday by visiting the Memorial that was built to honor him.

And in our homes and schools and churches we celebrate Lincoln's birthday by reading his words and remembering him—a great President and a great man.

ABOUT THE AUTHOR

Clyde Robert Bulla was born near King City, Missouri. He received his early education in a one-room schoolhouse where he began writing stories and songs. After several years as a writer of magazine stories, he finished his first book, then went to work on a newspaper.

He continued to write, and his books for children became so successful that he was able to satisfy his desire to travel through the United States, Mexico, Hawaii, and Europe. He lives in Los Angeles, California.

In 1962, Mr. Bulla received the first award of the Southern California Council on Children's Literature for distinguished contributions to the field of children's literature. He has written more than thirty stories for young readers.

ABOUT THE ILLUSTRATOR

Ernest Crichlow is both an illustrator and a painter; his works are represented in many private collections and in museums, galleries, and libraries throughout the United States. Mr. Crichlow was born in Manhattan. He has taught art at Shaw University, at St. Augustine College, and at the Waltann School. He lives in Brooklyn, New York.